To,052

WORLD ECONOMY EXPLAINED

The Stock Market

Sean Connolly

amicus

Published by Amicus
P.O. Box 1329
Mankato, MN 56002

Printed in the United States of America, at Corporate Graphics in North Mankato, Minnesota.

Library of Congress Cataloging-in-Publication Data

Connolly, Sean, 1956-
  The stock market / by Sean Connolly.
    p. cm. -- (World economy explained)
  Includes index.
  Summary: "Explains the functions and history of the stock market and its involvement with the 2007 credit crunch"--Provided by publisher.
  ISBN 978-1-60753-082-4 (hbk.)
  1. Stock exchanges--Juvenile literature. 2. Stocks--Juvenile literature. 3. Financial crises--Juvenile literature. I. Title.
  HG4553.C665 2011
  332.64'2--dc22

                                                          2009029073

Designed by Helen James
Edited by Mary-Jane Wilkins
Picture research by Su Alexander

Photograph acknowledgements
page 7 John Sturrock/Alamy; 9 American School/Getty Images; 10 Alex Inglis/Getty Images; 12 Mary Evans Picture Library/Alamy; 15 Visions of America, LLC/Alamy; 16 Time & Life Pictures/Getty Images; 19 Getty Images; 21 Philip Wolmuth/Alamy; 23 Peter Bowater/ Alamy; 24 Vario Images GmbH & Co.KG/Alamy; 27 Lebrecht Music and Arts Photo Library/Alamy; 29 L. Zacharie/Alamy; 31 Time & Life Pictures/Getty Images; 32 Photos 12/Alamy; 34 AFP/Getty Images; 36 Time & Life Pictures/Getty Images; 39 Orjan F. Ellingvag/Dagens Naringsliv/Corbis; 41 Nick Turner/Alamy; 43 London Photos-Homer Sykes/Alamy
Front cover John Sturrock/Alamy

DAD0039
32010

9 8 7 6 5 4 3 2 1

Contents

Politics and the Economy

In 1992, Bill Clinton became president of the United States, beating George H.W. Bush in the polls. Bush had already served one four-year term as president and had been confident that he would be re-elected. But he overlooked something very important—voters' confidence in how the next president would look after the economy.

The world had just emerged from a recession, and American voters were anxious about their savings, their ability to pay for health care, and their jobs. Clinton's team understood those concerns and summed up Bush's attitude with the phrase, "It's the economy, stupid."

Five years later, Britain elected Tony Blair as prime minister. Like the Americans in 1992, British voters voted out a political leader (the Conservative John Major) who was linked to bad economic times.

These cases show how political leaders are judged first and foremost by how well they look after their own people. The economy does lie at the heart of politics. In countries such as the United States and Britain, the economy depends on the success of companies in providing jobs, selling goods, and making money for themselves and the country.

A Stake in the Economy

Companies provide work and national income, but also offer people the chance to share in their success. People can buy a part, called a share, of a company to show their confidence in the company. When the company does well, or looks likely to do well in the near future, the value of these shares rises. On the other hand, when the outlook is bleak—for the company or the country as a whole—the share value falls.

People buy and sell shares in buildings called stock exchanges, and the term for this trading is called the stock market. When a stock market is healthy, the value of shares remains steady or rises. Falling prices show that people are losing confidence—either in a particular company or in the economy as a whole.

Stock markets lie at the heart of modern economies, because they can raise money for companies, and because they offer people a chance to invest money in these companies. Stock markets reflect how well the overall economy is performing, but they can also influence people's attitudes about the future. Sometimes stock markets can help to start a sluggish economy moving again. At other times, rapidly falling prices can produce a sort of panic that spreads throughout a country—and sometimes across the world.

This book explains how stock markets work and just how it is that buying and selling shares—which some people view as gambling—can affect everything in our lives.

Traders in colorful jackets check prices and make deals on the floor of the London Stock Exchange.

Taking Stock

Imagine setting up a small company to produce and sell jam. Some of the workers make the jam in batches; others pour it into jars. When the jam has cooled, another group tightens the lids, labels the jars, and packs them in boxes. The jars sell for $3, and the profit on each is $1.50. Using this method of production, the company sells 300 jars each week, making a profit of $450.

The company owner then discovers that if they used a machine to fill and seal the jars, the company could produce and sell 1,000 jars a week. The only problem is that the machine costs $15,000, and the company cannot afford to buy one. Then the owner has another idea: she will approach local people and see whether 150 of them would each pay $100 so the company can afford to buy the machine. The company would not pay them back directly, in the way it would pay back a loan. Instead, it would agree that each person who invested $100 would have a share in the future profits of the company. In effect, these people would become part owners of the company.

The original owner had to give up some of the control over the company as part of the deal, but he or she would still be better off under the new system. Within ten weeks, the company would have earned back the cost of the machine. After that, everyone would start to receive a share of the profits.

The History of Share Owning

This idea of sharing costs in the hope of sharing income is not a difficult one to understand. And although most companies—large or small—use such a system of raising money, the idea is not a new one, either. Some versions of this idea go back more than 700 years.

Those early versions, such as a thirteenth-century Swedish agreement under which people shared the costs and profits of running a mine, were called joint-stock companies.

The terms stock market and stock exchange come from the same root as joint stock. Companies still use the word stock to describe the goods they have—books, toys, cars, or even jam (as in the earlier example)—which they can sell to earn money. Joint-stock companies offered people the

This eighteenth-century illustration shows slaves harvesting tobacco in colonial Virginia. Slaves did all of the work, but had no share in the profit they helped produce.

chance to own some of the companies' stock in return for a share in the profits from sales. Of course, this ownership worked both ways: if a company went out of business or if its inventory were stolen or destroyed, then the investors would also lose their money.

The first important joint-stock companies grew up in England, Spain, the Netherlands, and in other European countries during the sixteenth and seventeenth centuries. European merchants had just begun sailing to Asia to buy spices, silks, china, and other goods that would fetch good prices in their home countries. Investors could share in these enormous profits, but they lost their money if company ships sank or were captured by enemy navies or pirates. Despite those risks, enough people found the profits attractive to continue investing.

Dawn of the Modern Era

Joint-stock operations such as the Virginia Company and the Plymouth Company were at the forefront of much of England's

Four major rail companies formed the Forth Bridge Company in 1873 to build a rail link across the Firth of Forth in eastern Scotland. The company raised almost $4 million (equivalent to $400 million today) for the building work, which lasted from 1882 to 1890.

Personal Account

TRADING BY FORCE

English traders and investors founded the East India Company in 1600 to benefit from the enormous potential of the Asian spice trade, especially in the countries now called India and Indonesia. The Dutch East India Company was established two years later and had the same goal—both of these joint-stock companies sought to eat into the trade Portugal and Spain had developed in Asia during the 1500s.

The English and Dutch competed with the Portuguese and Spanish, and many Europeans lost sight of the other trading partners—the Asians themselves. Their needs and wishes were swept aside as European merchants moved in to trade with them, whether the Asians wanted to trade or not.

The trading companies became almost as powerful as armies as they competed to make large Asian profits for their investors at home. A Dutch trader in Asia, Jan Pieterszoon Coen, wrote to his company's directors in 1614: "Trade in India must be conducted and maintained under the protection and favor of your weapons, and the weapons must be supplied from the profits enjoyed by the trade, so that trade cannot be maintained without war or war without trade."

exploration and settlement of North America. English investors were proud to see their flag flying in their colonies, but they were just as pleased with the profits they earned from North American tobacco, sugar, furs, and slave-trading.

By the middle of the seventeenth century, merchants gathered in London coffeehouses to discuss trading opportunities around the world. They were eager to make the best trades on more familiar goods such as wheat, sugar beets, and cattle. In 1698, a trader named John Castaing set up an exchange in Jonathan's, one of London's most popular coffeehouses. This was the first modern stock exchange, where deals could be done. After a bad fire in London in the eighteenth century, traders set up a bigger exchange for their trading. In 1801, it received the name the Stock Exchange. The modern era of trading had arrived.

How Stock Markets Work

Although people can now choose

from many different ways of investing their money, thanks to modern technology, at the simplest level investing in the stock market resembles the trading that took place in London's seventeenth-century coffeehouses.

Investors usually do not buy shares directly. Instead they use professionals called stockbrokers to do their trading for them. The brokers deal directly on a major stock exchange—such as London, New York, or Tokyo—and quote the current price for a share in a particular company. If an investor chooses to buy shares, the broker does the deal there and then for a certain number of shares at a certain price per share (or share price).

Listed or Unlisted

Presidents who decide to sell shares in their company usually choose between becoming a listed or unlisted company. A listed company offers its shares for sale to the general public—these companies are also known as public companies. The term listed means that a company is listed on a stock exchange. Unlisted companies also break down ownership into shares of the company's worth, but these companies only sell their shares to the presidents themselves.

Each of these choices has advantages and disadvantages. Listed companies can raise money—often very quickly—by offering more shares for sale. This freedom enables them to make quick decisions that could help the company, for example, to buy materials to produce an extra batch of goods quickly. But this ability to raise cash also comes at a cost—rivals could buy enough shares in a company to take over that company. Having a majority of shares can give a shareholder (either an individual or another company) power over the company.

Unlisted companies can't raise money quickly by selling shares to the public. But their presidents do keep control of their company and do not face the risk of what's called a hostile takeover. The main reason for having shares is so that the presidents can enjoy limited liability—this means that the presidents are responsible for only a certain sum of money (the value of their share in the company) if the company runs into trouble and builds up huge debts.

Opposite: This nineteenth-century bond certificate is proof that someone has invested in a company, in the same way as if they had bought shares. Companies use investors' bond money as though it has been loaned to them, and promise to repay it with interest.

The investor then pays the broker and receives a share certificate, which is proof of ownership of the shares that have just been bought. Becoming a shareholder gives an investor certain privileges. For example, shareholders can attend special meetings where they can vote on company matters, because they are, in effect, part owners of the company.

Shareholders also qualify for a share in the company's profits. Many companies divide some of these profits and distribute them to shareholders, either as cash (dividends) or in the form of more shares. Companies do not have to pay dividends. Many companies put their profits back into the company to help it grow. People investing in such companies might hope to see a return on their investment in the form of a rising share price (they can always sell some shares for a profit). Companies that pay out dividends tend to be more established; although their share price might not rise rapidly, investors can hope for a steady flow of dividends instead.

Getting It Straight

Because people can put their money in such a wide variety of investments, many terms have developed to describe special ways of buying, selling, saving for, or simply considering shares. And with new technology playing such a large part in the whole process, new terms are always being added.

To make matters even more confusing, Americans, the British, and other countries sometimes use terms that are not used elsewhere —or use the same term to mean different things. Perhaps the most common stumbling blocks for newcomers are the terms stocks and shares. British traders buy and sell part ownership (or shares) of companies. They use the word stock to mean a collection of these shares. Americans often use the term stocks instead of shares. This use of the term is older and more traditional and goes back to the idea of joint-stock companies (see pages 8–11).

Many countries use the term stock exchange to describe the place where the buying and selling takes place. The related term stock market refers more to the general feeling about whether prices are rising or falling in stock exchanges.

Opposite: Skyscrapers dwarf smaller buildings around Wall Street, the heart of New York City's financial district. Traders have been active on Wall Street for more than 200 years.

Financial Centers

Brokerages in most major cities are located near the major stock markets (or exchanges), and even people who know nothing about investment associate these neighborhoods with stocks and shares.

New York City's Wall Street is an area where most of the trading in stocks and shares takes place. Maps of the city list it as the financial district. Most people refer to it as Wall Street because it is one of the narrowest streets that cut through the tall skyscrapers of the city.

Other major cities around the world also have their own "Wall Streets." In London, the term "the City" refers to the district within the city of London that includes the London Stock Exchange and the many brokerage houses.

The Marketplace

Stock markets lie at the heart of many economies, especially those of the richest countries in the world such as the United States, the United Kingdom, and Australia. At the heart of the stock markets are the companies that raise their money in them. Without companies that seek to make a profit —attracting outside investors along the way—there would be no stock markets.

The economic system that allows companies to raise money—and individuals to invest—in this way is called capitalism or free enterprise. Capital is another word for funds such as money; such funds (earned,

Former U.S. Vice President Richard Nixon talks to Soviet leader Nikita Khrushchev at an international fair in Moscow in 1959. Nixon believed that American business—free to seek money from investors—provided better products.

invested, or sometimes lost) are at the center of the stock market system. Free enterprise describes the freedom that companies have to operate in this way, without the government interfering in what they do.

Stock markets control billions of dollars of investors' money, and the companies involved can provide jobs or investment income for many thousands of people. For these reasons, some economists believe that stock markets are the ideal system for creating wealth for the largest number of people. This view tends to be more common when stock markets are stable and earn their investors a good return on money invested through them.

Modern Attitudes

The 1980s was a stable period financially, and it paved the way for many of today's attitudes toward stock markets generally. The Cold War was coming to an end, and it seemed to many that the world could simply settle down to working hard and making money.

Political leaders, such as U.S. president Ronald Reagan and British prime minister Margaret Thatcher, encouraged people to invest in shares. These leaders believed that the 1980s boom in share prices would benefit everybody—even people who had no shares—because of all the extra jobs that would be created by growing companies. Just as importantly, they believed that the normal buying and selling of shares on the stock markets (sometimes called the marketplace) would keep the economy healthy in other ways.

People who held this view believed that a company that was badly organized or that made unpopular products would see its share price fall because people would not have confidence in its future. Instead, investors would put their money in healthier rival companies. President Reagan referred to this process as "the magic of the marketplace."

What Goes Up Must Come Down?

Stock markets offer people the chance to increase their money very quickly, provided they know when to buy and sell (or sometimes sell and buy back) shares. For example, if a person invested $10,000 in Apple, Inc. at the beginning of 2000 and sold those shares eight years later, he or she would have made a profit of $70,000. The Apple share price rose from $25 to $200, largely because Apple introduced the popular iPod during that time.

An investor who bought and later sold those shares might have been clever, believing that Apple was probably going to introduce a product that would sweep the world with its popularity. On the other hand, that person might just have been lucky, having decided to invest in the company because of the name.

Then there is the matter of deciding when to sell. Did the investor decide to buy a new house in 2008 and sell the Apple shares because the extra money would be useful? Or did the investor have the feeling that the world economy was heading for troubled times, and that all share prices—and not just Apple's—would fall dramatically in 2008? Either way the investor would have been fine, because the Apple share price dropped from $200 to about $75 during the course of 2008.

Others saw it less as magic and more like the scientific theory of natural selection, which is often called the survival of the fittest.

The British government led by Prime Minister Thatcher followed a wide-ranging policy of privatizing many companies that had been previously owned by the government. Critics (including some in Mrs. Thatcher's own Conservative Party) accused the government of "selling off the family silver." But Mrs. Thatcher and her supporters believed that the big companies would provide a better service if they were privately owned. She also believed that ordinary people would gain some power to influence the country if they owned shares in

YOUR MONEY'S WORTH

Foolish Investors

In his book Eat the Rich, *writer P.J. O'Rourke uses humor to explain how the world economy operates. This is his explanation of how buying stocks works: "You buy stocks because you think other people will think this stock is worth more later than you think it's worth now.*

"Economists call this the 'Greater Fool Theory.'" How accurate do you think this explanation is? If you don't agree with O'Rourke, how would you change his wording?

its major companies. She and her supporters believed in what they called a "share-owning democracy." By the end of the 1980s, about eight million people in the UK owned shares. That was three times more than had owned shares at the start of the decade. Those people would gain—or lose—along with the stock markets in the future.

Former UK Conservative Party leader Margaret Thatcher begins her party's successful election campaign in 1979. Thatcher's victory ushered in a new era of share ownership.

New Directions

Trading in stock markets has had the same goals for centuries. Companies issue shares to investors as a way of raising money and to fund the development of new products—or simply to grow. Investors expect shares either to provide them with a steady source of income over time, or to make money quickly.

Investors may also choose to put their money in bonds, which companies (and sometimes governments) issue as another means of raising money. The benefits of putting money into the stock market—either to build up a supply of money for retirement or possibly to make a large profit quickly—are still big attractions for investors. And the risk of losing everything because a company goes bankrupt or because the entire market crashes (see pages 24–27) would have been familiar to a seventeenth-century investor in the East India Company.

A New Era

The difference between trading today and centuries ago is that the modern stock market offers a bewildering number of investment choices. It also allows investors to pay for them by a variety of methods. The stock market has moved with the times: ticker tape (see page 30) was used rather than sending prices by messenger, then electronic pricing took the place of the ticker tape. Now computers streamline the whole process, making international trading not just possible but instant (see page 28). Investors, companies, and brokerage houses can use high-speed electronic payments to close deals or to make deposits.

Stockbrokers now refer to different types of investments as financial products. Some of these products, or methods of financing them, were originally designed to make life easier for ordinary investors. For example, techniques such as leveraging allowed people to borrow

Ethical Trading

British investors have invested about £4 billion ($6.6 billion) into what is called the ethical market. They put their money in funds that promise not to invest in any company or activity that might harm the environment, the world's people, or plants and wildlife. Some of these ethical funds go further by not simply avoiding "bad" companies, but actively supporting green or other ethical companies.

Others prefer to choose individual companies that they respect and invest in them directly rather than spreading their investments by using a fund. These investors study the business practices and trading histories of companies before making their decisions. The Ethical Investment Research Service (EIRIS) is a charity that monitors thousands of companies. It provides independent advice for investors —funds and individuals—who want to focus on using their money for positive change.

A worker on a family farm on the Caribbean island of Dominica prepares bananas for export as part of the Fairtrade organization that guarantees a fair price for farmers.

Back to Gold

When stock markets become unpredictable, many people take their money out of shares and invest in gold instead. This precious metal has been highly valued around the world for thousands of years. It also became the cornerstone of currency systems in many countries. Paper notes such as U.S. dollars, British pounds, and European euros could be converted into agreed amounts of gold. This system is called the gold standard.

National economies no longer use the gold standard with their currencies, but gold itself can be bought and sold, usually by the ounce.

And because people believe that gold holds its value, they turn to it when paper money and shares seem risky. As a result, the value of gold rises when the stock markets are in trouble and it falls again when shares start rising once more.

YOUR MONEY'S WORTH

A Price Worth Paying?

For many people, investment is all about return—how much their initial spending will grow over time. Many experts agree that companies involved with tobacco, alcohol, and weapons offer a better return than ethical companies.

Do you think a smaller return is the price ethical investors must be prepared to pay to stick by their principles? Or do you think that governments or stock markets should offer other advantages to attract investment in ethically responsible companies?

money to pay for shares, which would rise in value before the loan had to be repaid. Other techniques, such as using derivatives, involve complicated chains of linked investments. When times have been good —such as during the 1920s or the five years leading up to 2007—investors have benefited greatly from these methods. But when things go wrong, as they did in the recent credit crunch (see pages 32–35), they can make matters worse overall.

The lesson is that people should be careful and try to understand the risks as well as the promised returns of any investments they make.

Personal Account

TRADING IN SHARES

People can trade shares by computer, buying or selling shares simply by clicking on "Buy" or "Sell." The process is called day trading. Steve Bodow, an American writer, is one such amateur trader. He often spends hours at his computer, trading stocks and watching his earnings or losses change by the minute. He posted this typical account on wired.com, a technology news web site:

"We're braving the bear tide to buy an obscure company that goes by the symbol TRBD. We don't know what TRBD does, what it earns, even what its full name is. All we care about is whether the stock will, in the next five minutes, move fractionally up or down. DT, who's been following TRBD all day, says up… type 200 shares in one box, $8 per share into another, and click the 'Buy' button. Seconds later I own the stock. Hours later, when TRBD has coasted from $8 to over $10 a share, I click on 'Sell' instead of 'Buy.' The market's licking its wounds, but this afternoon I'm several hundred bucks in the black!"

Traders in traditional Arab clothing meet to discuss investments at the Dubai Financial Market, which acts as a stock exchange.

Bulls, Bears, and Bubbles

The stock market does not work along strict scientific lines despite what some of its defenders might claim. There are no guarantees that a company making excellent products at good prices will succeed. And there is no way of predicting when a company producing a silly product will make millions, and a handsome profit for its shareholders.

All sorts of factors play a part in the way stock markets operate. Some are unpredictable, such as the weather. For example, a severe frost that ruins the Spanish orange crop would drive down share prices of fruit-related companies. Other factors are not as unpredictable, but still fall

short of being certainties. The share price of the company that publishes the *Harry Potter* books around the world has risen and remained high throughout the history of the seven-book series, although other titles published by the same company may have been less succesful.

So it's always possible that people who invest in a company may experience unpleasant or pleasant surprises. But although they are surprises, there is always a chance that the outcome could be predicted. Frosts in orange-growing regions such as Spain are rare, but they do occur. Parents reading the first *Harry Potter* title could have judged that the books would be popular. Clever investors try to stay one step ahead of the market by selling orange-related shares at the first signs of cooler weather forecasts or buying shares in the publishers of *Harry Potter* after reading good reviews of the book.

Opposite: German shoppers wait to buy the seventh and final book in the Harry Potter *series, which has sold more than 400 million copies worldwide. This success has made author J.K. Rowling a billionaire and boosted the share price of her publishers.*

Other sudden rises or falls catch even the cleverest people unaware. One of the biggest-selling products in the 1970s was the Pet Rock. Gary Dahl, who worked in a California advertising company, bought a load of stones from a builders' supplier. Dahl set up a company, Rock Bottom Productions, and sold these stones in colorful boxes, as Pet Rocks. Inside the box was a set of instructions on how to train and care for the "pet." People thought the idea was funny and bought more than five million Pet Rocks over six months in 1975.

In the Mood

These failures and successes depend on the events related to specific companies, and not others. Unusual cold in Spain affects fruit growers and the companies that rely on them, but has little effect on car manufacturers, hotels, filmmakers, or any number of other industries. Similarly, *Harry Potter*'s success is confined to book publishers, makers of the *Harry Potter* films, and companies that produce toys based on the books and films. The Pet Rock was another one-off, an idea that had nothing to do with other companies.

Often, though, share prices rise or fall because most other shares are rising or falling. Investors develop what is described as a herd instinct, following each other's actions. Soon, a share price surge upwards or downwards can lead to an even sharper rise or fall. In a way, the market behaves like a single person, who is in either a good (positive) mood, or a bad (negative) mood. When the overall mood is positive and confident, people say there is a bull market. An overall negative investment mood leads to a bear market.

Sometimes this herd instinct can lead to an extremely fast rise, which often triggers an equally quick fall. The South Sea Bubble of 1720 in England is one famous case. In the space of a few months, the share price of the South Sea Company, which traded in South America, shot up to ten times its original value. The company had made wild claims about future success, so people rushed to buy shares, often borrowing heavily to pay for them. When the more down-to-earth truth emerged, the price dropped just as quickly, leaving many people penniless and resentful.

Many modern attitudes towards stock markets were formed after the Great Depression (see pages 32–34) caused a massive drop in share prices across

(see pages 32–34)

EXAMINATION CLOSER EXAMINATION **CLOSER EXAMINATION** CLOSER EXAMINATION CLOSER

The Original Bulls and Bears

Traders in stock markets have used the terms bulls and bears (referring to positive or negative feelings about prices) for more than 200 years. People disagree about how these animals became associated with shares. Some say it relates to the old European spectacle of watching bulls or bears fighting: bulls were said to swing their horns upward and bears slammed their paws downward. Others say it arose from the practice of fur traders, who often sold bearskins even before the bears were killed. This forward selling put pressure on huntsmen, leading to fears that they might not kill as many bears as the number of skins sold. According to this version, the word bull was added later to represent the opposite of the bear.

Personal Account

A JUDGEMENT?

Thomas Green, a bishop in England in 1721–1723, considered the collapse of the South Sea share price to be God's judgement on "the universal inclination of all ranks of men and women too to excessive gaming," which

brought "such a curse and blast upon us, as never was felt before by this Nation; by which we have been all of a sudden strangely impoverished in the midst of plenty, our riches having made themselves wings, and flying away nobody knows [where], and more families and single persons have been undone and ruined than hardly ever were known to have been so, by the most tedious and lingering war."

the world. After the Depression, which lasted about ten years, people were cautious about investing, and new regulations controlled stock market swings. But more than 80 years have passed since the Depression began, and some experts warn that people are forgetting the hard lessons that others learned then.

William Hogarth's satirical view of the South Sea Bubble shows London in chaos, with the Devil (on the left) laughing over the events of 1720.

The International Scene

Trading on stock markets is now truly
international. Today, because of time differences
around the world, trading never stops. When markets
are closing in the late afternoon in London or Paris,
New York City markets remain open for another five
hours. By the time New York City and other U.S.
stock markets close, those in Tokyo, Hong Kong, and
other Asian cities are opening for trading the next
day. As they close, European markets are reopening.

So trading really is a round-the-clock activity. This complex set
of markets around the world, each with an eye on the others, is a
reflection of something wider, called the global or world economy.

The advance of new technology, coupled with the growing number
of people in the world (which means more people to buy and sell
goods and services) have driven the huge progress. One of the most
important elements that drives this new international system is
stock market trading.

The Price of Progress?

The idea of a global economy is relatively new. Some people believe
it began at the end of World War I, as radio widened the scope of
instant communication. Others say it is a product of the computer
age, with instant trading now possible in any number of stock
markets around the world. Some experts look back further to the
eighteenth and nineteenth centuries, when European countries
established colonies in Africa, Asia, and the Americas. Raw materials
such as sugar, tea, and cotton from these colonies were shipped to
Europe, where companies manufactured products that were sold
and shipped around the globe again.

No matter how we define the beginning of the world economy, most people agree that stock markets—and national economies—are now linked in ways that would have been unthinkable in the past. For example, people in Germany can invest in a Japanese car-making company that produces some parts in Great Britain, others in Italy, and then assembles many of the cars in Spain. The success or failure of that Japanese company has enormous effects on the jobs and wealth of those other countries—and also affects the countries where the cars are sold.

America Sneezes

Stock markets around the world are in such close contact that the sort of swing that might once have happened in a single country —for example, the South Sea Bubble (see page 26)—can now spread across the globe almost instantly.

A Tokyo cyclist stops to check the latest share prices displayed on a bank window in Ginza, one of the city's prosperous neighborhoods.

Ticker Tape Parades

Buying or selling shares depends hugely on being up-to-date—knowing the exact price of a share at any moment. Otherwise, brokers and their customers would pay too much for some of their purchases or sell them for too little because the price had fallen or risen since the deal was made.

Until the middle of the nineteenth century, accurate deals could only be made in the exchanges themselves, where brokers could see the constantly changing prices that were posted. In 1867, the American inventor Edward A. Calahan developed a way of sending share information through the telegraph system. Information about shares—including their name, price, and whether the share price was rising or falling—was sent using Morse Code. Brokerage houses far from the center of trading then received this constant flow of information, which was tapped out on a moving stream of paper tape. The tap-tap sound of the share information being punched on the paper led to the nickname ticker tape. Huge piles of tape mounted up in the course of a business day.

Companies in New York City's financial district found a way to get rid of the ticker tape they used. They cut it into shreds, which were then thrown out of skyscraper windows on people passing by on the streets below. New Yorkers then started to use the ticker tapes in parades to celebrate happy occasions, such as the end of World War II, or to honor heroes.

New York City still holds ticker tape parades in the Canyon of Heroes (the narrow streets between the tall skyscrapers), even though information now travels via computers rather than ticker tape.

Even before the computer age, when people could already see important financial links between countries, business observers noted that there were strong ties between some countries. During the early part of the twentieth century, for example, the United States was emerging as the most powerful country in the world, especially in the world of business. Whether they liked it or not, people in other

Astronaut John Glenn was honored wth a ticker tape parade in New York City's financial district after completing one of the first American trips into space in 1962. The fragments of paper look like confetti.

YOUR MONEY'S WORTH

Stock Market Superpowers

Many economists believe that the age of American dominance in the business world is over or at least fading. They argue that China, India, and other growing countries will take over the role of leader in financial matters —a role that Britain played in the nineteenth century. Do you think that it is inevitable, or even a good thing, that one or two countries should have so much influence over the rest of the world?

countries had begun to depend on America—either as a market for their goods or as a source of investment in their companies. People acknowledged this link with sayings such as "America sneezes, and Europe catches a cold."

Some people argue that the age of the United States as a business superpower is over, and that other countries— especially those in Asia—are likely to be the new leaders. We can only wait and see.

The Credit Crunch

Since the middle of 2007, the world has been going through economic troubles which have puzzled, alarmed, and angered people. Banks, once symbols of respectability and caution, have gone out of business because they lent money carelessly for years. In 2007, the value of people's houses fell, making it difficult for their owners to sell them. Many companies lost money and had to lay off workers to stay in business.

YOUR MONEY'S WORTH

Another Depression?

Can you see any similarities between the Great Depression of the 1930s and the credit crunch of today? Do you think the world could slip into another depression? Why or why not?

Opposite: Unemployed New Yorkers line up for food during the Great Depression. Governments, traders, and the general public hope that the credit crunch will never be as bad as the global downturn of the 1930s.

Stock markets have picked up this feeling of gloom and uncertainty, so share prices have fallen even further and faster than house prices. Few experts agree on how serious this difficult period will be, or how long it will last.

Political leaders, who are elected partly to look after their countries' economies, have been reluctant to accept how serious the problems are, perhaps because they believed voters would blame them. Those leaders spent nearly a year, until well into 2008, trying to claim that the economic problems in their countries did not amount to a recession—and certainly not a depression.

The term that was coined and continues to be used to describe the global economic troubles is "credit crunch," because it appears that the problems began with poor banking decisions, and banks rely on credit (money) to operate smoothly. Lurking in the back of everyone's mind—even in the minds of people born decades after the event—is the Great Depression of the 1930s. Most people have seen the

stark images of that time, showing the soup kitchens that fed the unemployed, empty factories, stockbrokers without hope, and dusty farms where people could no longer afford to live.

Since the end of the Depression, stock markets around the world have used a number of safeguards. The goal of the safeguards is to protect the world against a recurrence of that terrible, damaging era. "It can't happen again," people say. "We've learned from our mistakes." Others argue that many of the factors that led to the Great Depression in the 1920s were echoed in the years leading up to the credit crunch. In their view, the first year of the credit crunch was ominously familiar.

A German trader at the Frankfurt Stock Exchange watches prices closely on October 13, 2008, after European leaders agreed to spend billions to help troubled banks.

The Role of the Stock Markets

Many who suffer financial difficulties do not care what they are called—they just want a fast solution. In the meantime, things seem uncertain, and this uncertainty extends to stock markets and their role.

Some people, especially those who believe in the magic of the marketplace (see pages 16–19), believe that stock markets can pull people—and even countries—up. They believe a period during which the value of shares goes up sends out new waves of confidence. For example, people with money to invest might be uncertain about whether to buy shares in a company that makes builders' vans. They might wonder whether the value of their investment would rise or fall. If the stock market rallied (or rose), then most share prices would rise. Some undecided people would invest. The boost from this new investment would raise the share price, which in turn could help to raise prices further, and so on.

This process, in which good news and positive results breed more success, is called a virtuous circle. A stock market that continues to rally can send out a message that it is time to take chances again—building offices, manufacturing cars, and opening branches of chain stores.

Every link in this chain adds jobs, and helps the country, possibly even the world, to start again.

Stock markets can also be seen as part of the problem, rather than part of the solution. Banks and their risky loans (particularly in the U.S.) set in motion the credit crunch, but that is only part of the picture. Some of the loans were risky—and likely to fail— because they were linked to complicated investment packages. Those packages tied together different investments, which included (in addition to high-risk mortgages) high-risk investments that were traded on the stock markets.

The stock-market investments were intended to spread the risk in case the mortgages were not repaid. Many were not repaid, but the stock markets could not cushion the blow. The scale of the mortgage failure made traders sell banking shares in panic. Instead of developing a virtuous circle to help resolve the crisis, the markets reflected just how bad things were. This view of stock markets sees them as producing a vicious circle, which makes recovery even harder because they drive prices (and people's confidence) down so quickly.

Getting a Grip

Since the first civilizations, people have tried to find the best system for looking after both well-being and wealth. The earliest societies were often based on physical strength or military power, with strong warriors controlling their neighbors. Eventually more advanced types of government developed, and kingdoms and empires grew along those lines. Strong rulers did not promise fairness; instead, they defended their people against invaders.

A taxi picks up a customer in the Czech capital, Prague, in 1956. Under communism, almost every way of earning a living —even driving a taxi— was controlled by the government.

Finding a Balance

Since about the sixteenth century, people have tried to form societies that offer security as well as the chance to build better lives for themselves through their own efforts. Capitalism (see pages 16–19), the system that developed stock exchanges, is one such way. Supporters of this system argue that it rewards individuals' efforts while making countries stronger.

Throughout more than three centuries of modern stock-market trading, some people have proposed other forms of society. The most important of these is communism. Instead of promising rewards to those who set up businesses, communist societies seek to give their citizens an equal share of the country's wealth—which means similar housing, pay, education, and medical care. All these are provided—and strictly controlled—by the government, and people have little individual freedom. Several countries adopted communist-style governments for much of the twentieth century. In many of these, citizens eventually decided that they would rather have the chance to run their own lives than have the basics handed out by the government.

By the early 1990s, most communist countries had adopted capitalist-style governments. The world's largest country, China, still claims to be communist, but it has also adopted many features of capitalism. By the beginning of the twenty-first century it seemed that the capitalist system had proved to be more popular than communism—but the present credit crunch has made many people reconsider whether this economic system really is the best and most efficient. Ordinary investors, members of the government, and even those involved in stock markets are asking whether there is some way of finding a balance.

YOUR MONEY'S WORTH

English Fair Play

In 1923, the London Stock Exchange was given its first coat of arms. It included the Latin motto dictum meum pactum, *which means "my word is my bond." This phrase reflected the pride that the exchange took in the honorable behavior of those who traded there. It also suggested that bad behavior would be quickly discovered, and the trader shamed into resigning. Do you think this motto still reflects the spirit of share trading? If not, why not?*

Different Approaches

Everyone who is interested in investing in the stock market expects fairness and accuracy. For example, they expect to receive accurate information before and after they make the decision to invest. Information about a company's performance (for example, how much money it expects to make or lose in the next year) is vital for decision-making. Traditionally, brokers and other stock-market traders operated on a system of trust. This system led to the motto of the London Stock Exchange (see page 37). At times, though, governments have stepped in and set up organizations to monitor trading and to make trading information public.

The U.S. Securities and Exchange Commission (SEC) was formed in 1934, at a time when American stock markets had slumped—and when they were suffering from a poor reputation. It is an independent part of the U.S. government and continues to enforce U.S. laws on finance and share trading.

The British have always resisted government involvement in stock markets. As a result, the Financial Services Authority (FSA), created in 2000, is independent of the British government and is funded by the companies and organizations it monitors. It is more of a watchdog than a legal enforcer, providing information and hearing complaints about financial services in all areas related to money —banks, insurance companies, mortgage lenders, and other organizations, as well as stock markets.

Can people still feel confident enough to set up their own business based on a good idea, or does the risk of losing everything in a stock market crash frighten people away? Can stock markets and governments find ways to protect investors without interfering with the "magic of the marketplace?" These questions continue to be asked, and in the meantime experts seek ways to find and enforce effective regulations to maintain the balance. It is a tricky process.

Bernard Madoff (center) was arrested in December 2008 and accused of masterminding the largest investment fraud in history. Thousands of investors lost up to $65 billion over nearly 20 years.

Personal Account

SPREADING CONFIDENCE?

Lord Adair Turner has been chairman of the Financial Services Authority (FSA) since September 2008. He assumed the post just as the full extent of the credit crunch was becoming clear. Five weeks into his new post, in an interview for the Guardian *newspaper*, an interviewer drew parallels between 2008 and the Great Depression of the 1930s.

Turner replied: "The past three weeks have been a very, very big watershed. It will take time to sink in that if more needs to be done it will be done. But there is no chance of a 1929–33 recession. We know the lessons and we know how to stop it happening again."

Looking Ahead

The dramatic events in the world of finance since 2007 have left many people uncertain about stock markets. In the world economy all countries are interlinked—what happens in one country often has an effect on the lives of people in other countries. The rise of new technology has made instant stock market transactions easier for ordinary investors. But perhaps one of the most important factors in people's attitudes is how involved people are in the stock markets themselves.

Direct Effects

In the past, many people felt that the ups and downs of world stock markets had no real effect on their lives. They could imagine stockbrokers becoming rich overnight, or ruined just as easily. But their own day-to-day lives seemed unaffected by stock markets. Some of the biggest financial crises, such as the Great Depression, alerted people to the role played by stock markets. But they could ignore the less dramatic stories of bull and bear markets.

That has changed over the past 20 or 30 years. More and more people around the world have a direct and immediate stake in stock markets—quite apart from feeling any side-effects of a downturn, such as unemployment or homelessness. About half of all American and British households own shares. Some of those shares are owned directly, for example the shares bought by people during the privatization of many British state-owned companies during the 1980s. These people continue to follow the stock market.

Households are also involved in less obvious ways. More people are investing in retirement or pension funds, to build up extra money

East European workers harvest cabbages on a British farm in 2002. With Britain braced for more economic trouble, few can predict where these workers will find themselves in the future —or what will happen to the world economy.

for when they stop working. These plans promise extra earnings for customers by investing their money in the stock market. Pension and retirement fund managers are renowned for their caution. They tend not to invest in companies that are very risky. Often they try to spread the risk by investing in a wide variety of companies. So, if one of the companies suffers a downturn, the gains in the other investments absorb the loss. For example, the share price of some carmakers

Personal Account

BEWARE OF GREEN SHOOTS

Justin Urquhart Stewart, a stock market expert, was interviewed in late 2008 about the credit crunch and the future. His views show the importance of the links between areas of finance which cause or solve problems.

"We've seen a restriction on credit. That's the lifeblood of capitalism. If you don't have enough credit, it's like cutting off the blood supply to your arm. It's slightly more than pins and needles—it's very painful… Personal finance debt is quite astonishing… You find that 25 percent of people's salaries is going just on servicing debt. That has to be worked through. Maybe this time next year, we'll be seeing some green shoots of things appearing as we've got through the bad news. But beware of green shoots—some of them turn into advanced mold."

can fall when the price of gasoline rises; owning other shares—with nothing to do with cars—spreads the risk and may offset any losses.

That system has benefited many people for more than 20 years, but the recent drop in share prices has affected the whole stock market. It is becoming harder to spread the risk, and people are thinking twice about investing in stocks and shares.

The Future

The global economy is tied together in some other ways, apart from the global links between stock markets and countries. Different areas of finance are also connected, for better or worse. For example, the credit crunch began as a banking problem but soon spread into the stock market because some of the banking problems were buried in traded investments.

Future regulators may need to address these links more directly. Individual countries such as the United States have already taken prompt (and costly) action to safeguard the banking industry. They expect that the return of calm banking operations will automatically spread to shares and other financial areas. Those dramatic reactions have brought criticism from different quarters. Some people in the investment world believe that companies or entire areas of investment should be allowed to sink or swim on their own, without help from governments. And some taxpayers resent seeing government money spent on protecting bankers and other financial people whose mistakes or poor judgement caused the problems in the first place.

Lively crowds at the annual London carnival reflect the international nature of major world cities.

YOUR MONEY'S WORTH

A Middle Way?

Can you think of a way of improving the system where stock exchanges operate so that they behave responsibly at the same time as offering companies the chance to raise money easily and providing investors with the chance to make money?

Think of the alternatives: less controlled stock markets are likely to have big swings up and down (with the chance of making or losing lots of money quickly) whereas strictly controlled markets might stifle people's willingness to set up, or invest in, companies.

Glossary

bear market   A period when share prices fall, and people expect them to fall further.

bond   A type of loan used by governments or large companies to raise money; investors buy a certain number and are promised repayment with interest.

boom   A period of economic growth and well-being.

bull market   A period when share prices rise, and people expect them to rise further.

capitalism   An economic system in which companies are run by private owners for profit, rather than owned by the state.

Cold War   The time from 1945 to 1990 during which the U.S. and other capitalist countries were hostile to communist countries, but not openly at war with them.

colony   A region controlled and governed by another country.

communism   A political system in which all property is owned by the community, and each person contributes and receives according to their ability and needs.

depression   A period of extreme financial difficulty, when many companies go out of business, and people lose their jobs.

derivative   A complicated investment that has a value linked to other factors, such as the general level of the stock market.

economist   Someone who studies how the economy operates.

ethical   Concerned with right and wrong.

forward selling   A sale price agreed in the present for delivery of something in the future.

fraud   A dishonest deal that cheats the government, a company, or people.

free enterprise   An economic system where private companies compete with each other and are not controlled by the state.

funds   Either a general term to describe money and other forms of payment, or a type of savings plan that spreads people's money across a wide range of investments.

gold standard   A system of operating a national currency so that the value of money is linked to specific amounts of gold.

Great Depression   The time of severe world economic difficulties, 1929–1939.

interest   The extra amount that a borrower pays back on a loan.

joint-stock company   A company whose stocks are owned jointly by its shareholders.

leverage   Using borrowed money to buy stocks or make other investments.

limited liability   A limited liabiity company makes the shareholders responsible only for the amount of money they have invested in it.

listed (of a company) Having shares that can be bought and sold in the stock market.

mortgage A sum of money that someone borrows from a bank to buy a house.

natural selection A scientific term describing how only the strongest or most adaptable living things survive and reproduce.

pension A regular sum of money paid to someone who has stopped working.

privatize To sell shares in a company that is owned by the government.

profit The amount a company receives minus the cost of supplying goods or services.

rally A term describing a time when share prices begin to rise after a fall.

recession A period of severe economic decline lasting six months or more.

share certificate An official document giving proof of ownership of a share or shares.

shareholder Someone who owns shares in a company.

stock exchange A place where shares and other investments are bought and sold.

unlisted (of a company) Having shares that can only be bought and sold privately, and not in a stock market.

vicious circle A situation in which one negative action leads to other negative outcomes, causing things to continue in the same way.

virtuous circle A situation in which one positive action leads to other positive outcomes, making it easier to continue in the same way.

watershed An important dividing line or turning point.

Further Reading

The Credit Crunch (The World Today) Colin Hynson (Sea-to-Sea, 2009)

Shares Made Simple: A Beginner's Guide to the Stock Market Rodney Hobson (Harriman House, 2007)

America in the 1930s (The Decades of the Twentieth Century) Edmund Lindop (Twenty-First Century Books, 2010)

Web Sites

Ethical Investment Research Service (EIRIS)
www.eiris.org

The Mint: Information on the Stock Market for Kids
http://www.themint.org/kids/
what-is-the-stock-market.html

PBS Video: The Ascent of Money
http://www.pbs.org/video/video/1170821435/
chapter/4/search/great%20depression

The New York Stock Exchange Web Site
http://www.nyse.com/

Index